The Publishers gratefully acknowledge assistance provided by Mrs Penelope Zapoleon, C.B.E., Mother Superior at MEDEA (The Maternal Educational Authority), in compiling this book.

Publishers: Ladybird Books Ltd., Loughborough

Printed in England. If wet, Italy.

'How it works'

THE
MUM

by J. A. HAZELEY, N.S.F.W.
and J. P. MORRIS, O.M.G.

(Authors of '101 Dog's Eggs')

A LADYBIRD BOOK FOR GROWN-UPS

This is a mum.

A mum has two very important jobs to do. One is to look after her children.

The other is to do everything else as well.

Being a new mum is full of wonder.

Sally wonders if her left shoulder will ever stop smelling of sick.

Gemma is having a little brother or sister for Shannon.

Gemma looks at all Shannon's old baby things and laughs. It seems so long ago. She has forgotten everything about babies.

This may be why she is having another one.

The mum gets lots of help from her little ones.

Daisy is helping to move the laundry basket away from her mum.

She has done this fourteen times in the last five minutes.

Eleanor and Simon have booked their first ever baby–sitter. They have a whole night to themselves.

They go to a restaurant and talk about whether the baby–sitter can cope if anything goes wrong

The baby–sitter will be slightly annoyed when Simon and Eleanor come home at nine o'clock.

Liz promised Oliver he could have some Tangfastics if he stopped screaming in the supermarket.

She was so embarrassed that she left before buying any real food.

Liz tells herself that, if she put the Tangfastics on a plate with enough tomato ketchup, they probably count as a vegetable.

The mum has sensitive ears which respond to the frequency of her child's voice.

The mum does not like hearing her own voice. That is because it does not sound like her voice any more.

It sounds like her mum's.

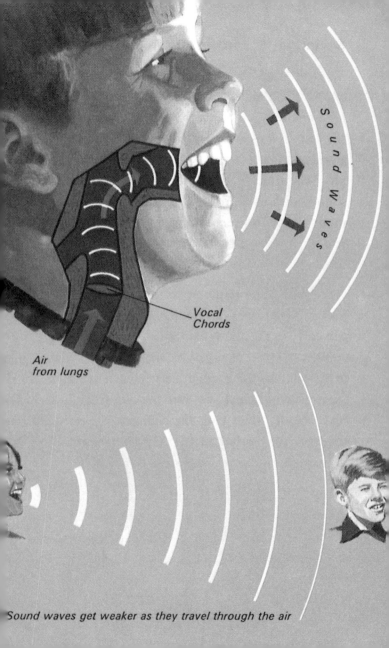

Sound Waves

Vocal Chords

Air from lungs

Sound waves get weaker as they travel through the air

Bella has made a den out of the clothes airer.

Bella's mum does not need the airer. She has been too busy doing things for Bella to wash any clothes.

Bella's mum wonders what the record is for the number of days someone has worn the same bra.

The mum is good at making thing
from whatever is lying aroun
the house.

Cathy made this dolly from th
corks of six bottles of Pinot Grigi
that were lying around the hous

One of the things that is no
lying around the house is her.

Now Lyndsay's little boy is a nursery, she is looking for a job

At this interview, the lady ask Lyndsay all sorts of questions which Lyndsay has troubl answering because she has th Octonauts theme going roun her head.

Lyndsay hopes she is not singin it out loud.

Alice is a successful biochemist. She publishes at least one highly regarded academic paper a year and has won the Colworth Medal.

At the school gate, nobody knows this. Alice does not even have a name. Everyone calls her Olivia's Mum.

Olivia has not done anything yet

Heather hoped she might be like the mum in one of the fairy—tales she read as a little girl.

But she is not good, gentle and kind. She is weary, waspish and resentful, like a wicked old step-mother.

Still, she did get one thing right. Everything in her home is covered in porridge.

Mums are everywhere.

In 1974, the Soviet Space Agency landed a robot mum on the moon

MAMA was designed to collect dust from the moon's surface using a reinforced silicon hanky and distilled spit.

Lily's mum says waiting for things makes them better. She says Lily can have the toy car if she waits until Christmas.

Lily does not mind. She is spending this weekend with her dad. She will get the car then.

On Sunday nights, Lily learns all sorts of interesting new words from her mum.

The mum always carries a handbag. It contains important supplies and weighs as much as a microwave oven full of shoes.

Fran has a recurring nightmare in which the Handbag Police caution her for not having enough wet wipes or emergency bananas.

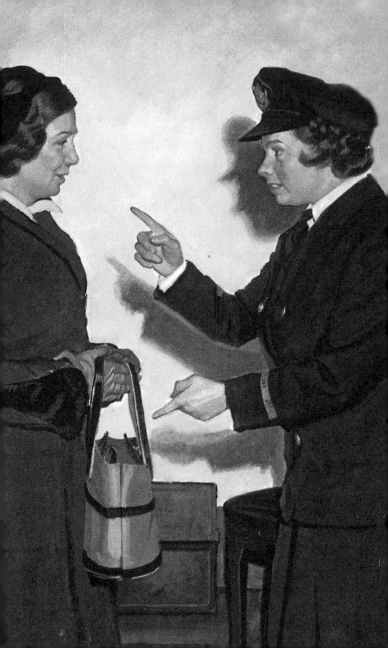

Sophie's son Ted has invited som
friends round for a birthday tea

Afterwards, Sophie finishe
the children's left-overs. Sh
is so full of ham, carrot-stick:
pitta bread, dips and cak
that she cannot bend ove

When Ted's dad comes home wit
a take-away curry, Sophie put
on her what-a-lovely-surpris
face and pretends to be ill.

Louise's cup of tea is going cold.

There are six other cold cups o
tea on surfaces round the house

When the vacuuming is done
Louise hopes she will be able to
find the time to throw them away

Julie said her children could have some pets if they promised to feed and look after them.

She has been too busy chasing Fluffy and Minecraft the lizard round the garden to get anything for supper.

'Lizard probably tastes a bit like chicken,' thinks Julie.

When she was single, Debbie had nightmares about being left alone and unwanted.

For the last three years, someone has called for her every two minutes and watched her every time she has taken a bath or sat on the toilet.

Debbie now dreams of being left alone and unwanted, even for just a few minutes.

Tara's sister has come for dinner. She is talking about American television programmes.

Tara has not seen any of the programmes her sister likes. This is because she goes to bed half an hour after the children.

She has seen Thomas and the Magic Railroad two hundred and eleven times, but she does not want to talk about it.

'Don't forget your scarf, Scott,' says his mum.

Scott has not forgotten his scarf in years. He is 46.

Lisa has been shopping. She had a long list of things to buy, but now thinks she may have forgotten something.

Lisa is right. She has forgotten her daughter. She left her playing on an iPad in Argos an hour ago.

Her daughter will still be there. She likes the iPad because it is not too busy to play with her.

The young kangaroo lives with its mum until it is strong enough to leave.

Unlike a human child, it does not move back in shortly afterwards and stay for years.

Philippa is cycling to work. She has already been awake for four hours because her two—year—old thinks wake—up time is 3.30am.

The other mums at work will have lots of reassuring stories about how their children sleep through and have to be woken for school.

Luckily, Philippa is too tired to kill the other mums.

THE AUTHORS would like to record their gratitude and offer their apologies to the many Ladybird artists whose luminous work formed the glorious wallpaper of countless childhoods. Revisiting it for this book as grown-ups has been a privilege.

MICHAEL JOSEPH

UK | USA | Canada | Ireland | Australia
India | New Zealand | South Africa

Michael Joseph is part of the Penguin Random House group of companies whose addresses can be found at global.penguinrandomhouse.com
First published 2016

004

Printed in Italy by L.E.G.O. S.p.A

A CIP catalogue record for this book is available from the British Library

ISBN: 978-0-718-18421-6

www.greenpenguin.co.uk

MIX
Paper from
responsible sources
FSC® C018179

Penguin Random House is committed to a sustainable future for our business, our readers and our planet. This book is made from Forest Stewardship Council® certified paper.